pray, praise, and give thanks

A Collection of Litanies, Laments, and Thanksgivings at Font and Table

GAIL RAMSHAW

 AUGSBURG FORTRESS

PRAY, PRAISE, AND GIVE THANKS
A Collection of Litanies, Laments, and Thanksgivings at Font and Table

Editor: Robert Farlee
Cover art: *Veiled Orante*, Catacomb of Priscilla, Rome
Cover design: Laurie Ingram
Book design: Tory Herman

ISBN 978-1-5064-1825-4

The paper used in this publication meets the minimum requirements of American National Standards for Information Sciences-Permanence of Paper for Printed Library Materials, ANSI Z329.48-1984.

Manufactured in U.S.A.
24 23 22 21 20 19 18 17   1 2 3 4 5 6 7 8 9

Contents

Acknowledgments 5

PRAYING TOGETHER 7

LITANIES AND LAMENTS
Praying with Litanies and Laments: An Introduction 10
A Litany of Praise for Creation 12
A Litany of Thanks for the Human Race 14
A Litany of Sorrows and Sins 16
A Template for the Prayers of Intercession 20
Lamenting Disease and Infirmity 22
Lamenting Injustices in Society 23
Lamenting Damage to the Earth 24
Lamenting the Grip of Melancholy 25
Lamenting the Dread of Mortality 26
Lamenting the Weight of Guilt 27

THANKSGIVINGS AT THE FONT
Praises at the Font: An Introduction 28
Water! Water! 30
Thanksgiving for the Waters of Baptism 32
Thanksgiving at the Font in a Time of Flood or Drought 34
Thanksgiving at the Font with Children 36

THANKSGIVINGS AT THE TABLE
Giving Thanks at the Table: An Introduction 37
For Advent 40
For Christmastide 42
For Epiphany and Transfiguration 44
For Lent 46
For Maundy Thursday 48
For the Resurrection of Our Lord: Easter Day 50
For Pentecost and Spirit Festivals 52
For Trinity Sunday: Triple Praise 54
For All Saints 58
For the Reign of Christ the King 60
A Eucharistic Prayer Inspired by Matthew 62
A Eucharistic Prayer Inspired by Mark 64

A Eucharistic Prayer Inspired by Luke 66
A Eucharistic Prayer Inspired by John 68
A Eucharistic Prayer after Catherine of Siena 70
A Eucharistic Prayer after Julian of Norwich 72
A Eucharistic Prayer after Martin Luther 74
An Earth Eucharistic Prayer 76
Thanksgiving in a Time of Communal Lament 78
A Variable Eucharistic Prayer 80

Image Credits 82

Acknowledgments

"For Advent" was written in 2011 at the request of the Rev. Amandus Derr, pastor of Saint Peter's Lutheran Church, New York City.

"For Epiphany and Transfiguration" was written in 2014 at the request of the Rev. Kevin Strickland, executive for worship, Evangelical Lutheran Church in America.

"For Maundy Thursday" was written in 2012 at the request of Scott Weidler, a member of the worship staff of the Evangelical Lutheran Church in America.

An early version of "For Resurrection Day" was included in the 1975 publication *The Great Thanksgiving*, released as part of the preparation of *Lutheran Book of Worship*.

"For Pentecost and Spirit Festivals" was written in 2015 at the suggestion of the Rev. Dr. Nelson Rivera, professor of systematic theology at the Lutheran Theological Seminary, Philadelphia.

"For the Reign of Christ the King" was written in 2011 at the request of the Rev. Robert Buckley Farlee, for use at Christ Church Lutheran, Minneapolis.

"A Eucharistic Prayer Inspired by Luke" was written in 2015 at the suggestion of the Rev. David Gambrell, editor of *Call to Worship*, a worship resource of the Presbyterian Church (USA).

"A Eucharistic Prayer Inspired by John" was written in 2016 at the request of the Rev. Kevin Strickland, executive for worship, Evangelical Lutheran Church in America, for first use at its 2016 Churchwide Assembly.

"An Earth Eucharistic Prayer" was first published in *Worship* 89 (2015) in the article "Liturgical Considerations of the Myth of Eden" (pp. 64–79), with the kind support of Bernadette Gasslein.

"A Eucharistic Prayer after Catherine of Siena," inspired by the Rev. Dr. Thomas McGonigle, O.P., is composed of phrases from the prayers of ecstasy in *The Prayers of Catherine of Siena*, numbers 5, 10, 11, 12, 17, and 19, as translated and edited by Suzanne Noffke, O.P. (New York: Paulist, 1983), and are cited with Noffke's kind permission.

"A Eucharistic Prayer after Julian of Norwich" is composed of phrases from Julian of Norwich's *Revelations of Divine Love*, with the kind assistance of Elaine Julian Ramshaw.

For this collection of prayers, I am indebted to the following mentors and editors: Daniel Brockopp†, Alexander Schmemann†, Robert Jenson, Gabe Huck, Bernard Benziger, Eugene Brand, Samuel Torvend, Frank Stoldt, Suzanne Burke, Scott Weidler, Miriam Schmidt, David Gambrell, Bernadette Gasslein, Benjamin Stewart, and, most especially, Robert Buckley Farlee, Martin Seltz, and Kevin Strickland. For thirty years I have received gracious critique of my work from Gordon Lathrop, to whom I offer my continuous and joyous gratitude.

praying together

Each Sunday and throughout the week, Christians assemble as Mater Ecclesia—mother church. She stands in *orans*, opening her palms in praise and petition to God, and extending her arms to embrace the community. As she—that is, the assembly—prays, so we come to believe.

Because of the import of this worship, Christians are intentional about the content and quality of their communal prayers. In some denominations, the desire for excellent prayer has meant that only those texts that have been officially crafted and ecclesially authorized are acceptable for use in the liturgy. On the other hand, some denominations judge that the very process of the prior printing of a prayer restricts the Holy Spirit, and so all corporate prayers at public worship are to be extemporaneous.

Some denominations, including most Lutherans, Presbyterians, Methodists, Episcopalians, and united Protestant communions, are between the ends of this continuum. These churches or their publishing houses dedicate considerable energy into crafting, approving, and distributing prayers for worship, while also allowing, perhaps even encouraging, local assemblies to adapt official prayers or to craft new prayers appropriate to the specific liturgical setting. It is especially for the assemblies in these denominations that the prayers in *Pray, Praise, and Give Thanks* are offered. For other denominations, these texts can provide inspiration.

This collection includes three categories of prayers: litanies and laments for a variety of worship situations, including a template for the Sunday intercessions; thanksgivings at the font of baptism; and thanksgivings at the table of holy communion. Because many denominations maintain the classic Western tradition of assembly prayer, these texts utilize historic outlines, familiar biblical references, and well-known responses. The usual practice of including the biblical narrative of the last supper within the text of the eucharistic prayers has been retained.

Yet these prayers are situated outside the usual ecclesial style of prose. Many of these prayers include diverse images of God. Each prayer attempts something new, an idea beyond the agenda of overworked committees, or an expression of a current theological proposal. One example of such an innovation deals with the matter of address: In the standard liturgical texts of the Western church, it has been traditional to address prayers to God the Father, through the Son, and in the Spirit. Some prayers in this collection adopt a pattern more usual in the Eastern church, in which the whole Trinity is addressed in liturgical prayer.

Who am I, a Lutheran laywoman, to craft these prayers? In 1965 I complained to my university's chaplain about some Sundays' intercessions and soon after was hired to prepare prayers for collegiate worship. In the fifty years since, I have crafted many prayers, and the approval and encouragement that I have received have persuaded me to seek publication of this selection of texts. Many of these prayers have been improved by the suggestions made by colleagues and friends or were altered after first use in worship.

A CD-ROM has been bound into the back of this book so that with ease and accuracy you can insert these copyrighted prayers into your leader's binder. If you choose to print prayers in service folders, please consider replacing sections of the texts with ellipses, thus keeping assembly worship from becoming an exercise in reading. Perhaps only cue lines need to be provided. In some prayers, the assembly's response repeats the presider's words, and for these phrases, whether spoken or sung, only a beckoning gesture from the presider is necessary. Respect for the author and adherence to the law remind users to cite this source somewhere in any disseminated text. One advantage of not distributing a printed text is that the prayers can be more freely adapted for your community and its needs. In this volume, explanatory material, rubrics, and fill-ins are indicated in italics. Brackets denote optional passages. Assembly responses are printed in bold type.

In 1960 my confirmation verse was Psalm 34:3: "Proclaim with me the greatness of the LORD; let us exalt God's name together." Welcome to this collection of prayers. May it supplement your resources and enrich the worship of your assembly.

litanies and laments

Praying with Litanies and Laments: An Introduction

A litany is a time-honored format for communal prayer, in which a leader speaks an extended text to which the assembly offers a simple repetitive response. This collection includes three litanies. The Litany of Praise for Creation gives thanks to God for the created earth, using the poem in Genesis 1 as its outline. The Litany of Thanks for the Human Race blesses God for the vast diversity within humankind. The Litany of Sorrows and Sins begs God for mercy and asks for God's deliverance from afflictions. These litanies may find use in Sunday worship or in a variety of other devotional settings. A template for the most common litany, that of the Sunday intercessions, is provided.

Christian communities are accustomed to praying for forgiveness, and many appropriate texts are at hand. But recently many Christians have sought texts for other matters of communal lament, and such texts are less readily available. This collection offers six participatory texts with a common format. As need suggests, assemblies may join in praying one of these laments, either in the gathering rite in Sunday worship, as part of the weekly intercessions, or in a devotional setting. Each lament cites a biblical story of salvation and addresses one of the following concerns: disease and infirmity, the injustices in society, ecological damage, the negative force of melancholy, the dread of death, or the weight of guilt.

Mark 2:4 tells of those who opened up a hole in the roof of a house so as to lower a paralyzed man to Jesus. The hope is that these texts will assist your assembly as it presents the needs of the world to God.

Litany of Praise for Creation

This litany is inspired by the poem in Genesis 1.

Glory to you, O God:
you speak a word of power,
and so you create the world.
We praise you, O God:
We praise you, O God.

For the Spirit hovering to bring forth life,
for the earth ordered from chaos,
and for light and dark,
we bless you, O God:
We bless you, O God.

For the cosmos beyond our earth,
for the sky above our heads,
and for the cycle of evening and morning,
we exalt you, O God:
We exalt you, O God.

For the seas, the lakes, and the rivers,
for the land with its mountains and plains,
and for the trees, the plants, and their fruits,
we magnify you, O God:
We magnify you, O God.

For the sun to rule the day,
for the moon to brighten the night,
and for the shining stars,
we extol you, O God:
We extol you, O God.

For the fish in the sea,
for the birds of the air,
and for the monsters in the deep,
we glorify you, O God:
We glorify you, O God.

For wild animals and creatures of all kinds,
for cattle and all livestock,
and for everything that creeps on the earth,
we adore you, O God:
We adore you, O God.

For humankind made in your image,
for setting us on your good earth,
and for providing us food to eat,
we worship you, O God:
We worship you, O God.

Bless us, your creatures.
Accept our praise,
and make us worthy of your marvelous creation.
We praise you, O God:
We praise you, O God.

Blessing and glory and wisdom and thanksgiving
and honor and power and might
be to you, our God, forever and ever.
Amen.
Amen.

A Litany of Thanks for the Human Race

Glory to you, O God, for creating the human race
and for endowing us with the mystery of your image.
We praise you, O God:
We praise you, O God.

For Africans and Asians and Indians,
for Australians and Europeans and Americans,
and for tribal peoples and island dwellers,
we bless you, O God:
We bless you, O God.

For blacks and whites and yellows,
for browns and reds and those in between,
and for their children of every hue,
we exalt you, O God:
We exalt you, O God.

For Hindus and Buddhists and Muslims,
for Jews and Christians and all God-fearing people,
and for all who care for the earth and for one another,
we magnify you, O God:
We magnify you, O God.

For newborns and toddlers,
for children and youth,
and for adults and the aged,
we extol you, O God:
We extol you, O God.

For the healthy and the infirm,
for the worker and the owner,
for those we admire and those we fear,
we glorify you, O God:
We glorify you, O God.

For persons who lead,
for persons who follow,
and for those who walk alone,
we adore you, O God:
We adore you, O God.

To all the human family,
Make us a blessing.
We bless you, O God:
We bless you, O God.

Blessing and glory and wisdom and thanksgiving
and honor and power and might
be to you, our God, forever and ever.
Amen.
Amen.

A Litany of Sorrows and Sins

Have mercy, O God:
Have mercy, O God.

Hear our lament, tenderhearted God.
Receive our petitions, benevolent God.
Forgive us our sins,
preserve us from evil,
and protect us in death.
Support us, mighty God:
Support us, mighty God.

We have honored false gods,
desecrated your name,
devalued worship,
disdained our elders,
harmed both neighbors and nature,
misused sexuality,
cheated and stolen,
lied and slandered,
and coveted what you have given to others.
Forgive us, loving God:
Forgive us, loving God.

From wrecking your creation,
from contaminating space,
from polluting the air,
from endangering the animals,
from abusing the soil,
from harming the plants,
and from fouling the waters,
deliver us, merciful God:
Deliver us, merciful God.

From nuclear destruction,
from war between the nations,
from strife within our country,
from political repression,
from prejudice and injustice,
from riots in our streets,
and from domestic violence,
rescue us, gracious God:
Rescue us, gracious God.

From plague and disease,
from hunger and thirst,
from injury and infirmity,
from unemployment and homelessness,
from ignorance and despair,
from loneliness and fear,
and from early or painful death,
protect us, compassionate God:
Protect us, compassionate God.

Loving God, merciful, gracious, compassionate,
remember your promise to save:
remember Cain, saved from revenge;
remember Noah, saved from the flood;
remember Sarah, saved from childlessness;
remember Hagar, saved from thirst;
remember the Israelites, saved from slavery;
remember Ruth, saved from starvation;
and remember Naaman, saved from disease.
Remember your promise, O God:
Remember your promise, O God.

Loving God, merciful, gracious, compassionate,
we are the needy:
we are Adam and Eve, expelled from the garden;
we are Joseph, abandoned by his brothers;
we are the slaves, pleading for freedom;
we are Miriam, struck with leprosy;
we are David, mourning our children;
we are Jeremiah, alone in the pit;
and we are Esther, begging for justice.
Save the needy, O God:
Save the needy, O God.

We implore you, faithful God, to receive our petitions,
as you hear the prayers of your Son,
as you heed the groaning of your Spirit.

Have mercy, O God:
Have mercy, O God.

Have mercy, O God:
Have mercy, O God.

Have mercy, O God:
Have mercy, O God.

A Template for the Prayers of Intercession

This template assists in the crafting of comprehensive intercessions.

With the whole people of God in Christ Jesus,
let us pray for the church, those in need, and all of God's creation.

We pray, holy God, for the church universal—
    for the unity of the church
        for _____*the national and regional church*_____ ,
        for _____*a church community in the news*_____ ,
        for _____*our local parish leaders by name or title*_____ ,
        for . . . _____ ,
    O God, our Sanctuary, empower the church, and in your mercy,
hear our prayer.

We pray, omnipotent God, for the well-being of creation—
    for the will and wisdom to care for the earth
        for _____*lands facing climate change*_____ ,
        for _____*local waters*_____ ,
        for _____*a species of endangered animals*_____ ,
        for . . . _____ ,
    O God, Rainbow of promise, preserve the earth, and in your mercy,
hear our prayer.

We pray, righteous God, for peace and justice in the world—
    for efforts toward international cooperation
        for peace in _____*countries in conflict or at war*_____ ,
        for an increase of justice _____*in a nation or a current situation*_____ ,
        for _____*our elected officials by name or title*_____ ,
        for . . . _____ ,
    O God, Sovereign and Judge, guide the nations, and in your mercy,
hear our prayer.

We pray, benevolent God, for the poor, oppressed, sick, bereaved, lonely—
    for the hungry and the homeless
    for persons without family or friends
        for _____*a group of the distressed in the news*_____ ,
        for _____*those afflicted with some disease or debility*_____ ,
        for . . . _____ ,
    O God, Shepherd and Mother, protect the needy, and in your mercy,
hear our prayer.

We pray, compassionate God, for all who suffer in body, mind, or spirit—
    for those in hospitals and other institutions of care
    for those who have no medical care
    for those who are incarcerated
    for _____ *names of the sick* _____ ,
    for . . . _____ ,
    for all who today will die—
    O God, Healer and Nurse, heal the sick, and in your mercy,
hear our prayer.

We pray, faithful God, for our congregation—
    for deeper faith and stronger commitment for us all
    for our homebound members
    for _____ *an outreach program* _____ ,
    for _____ *an internal matter* _____ ,
    for . . . _____ ,
    O God, Everlasting Arms, embrace this assembly, and in your mercy,
hear our prayer.

We pray, loving God, for the desires of our hearts—
    (keep five seconds of silence—)
    O God, our Heart's Desire, grant us peace, and in your mercy,
hear our prayer.

Receive our thanksgiving, eternal God, for all who have died in the faith—
    for _____ *the faithful departed on the commemorations list who died near this date* _____ ,
    for _____ *any renowned Christian who died this past week* _____ ,
    for _____ *congregation members who died this past week* _____ .
    That at the end we will join with them to rejoice in your presence,
    O God, our Homeland, gather us to yourself, and in your mercy,
hear our prayer.

Into your hands, gracious God, we commend all for whom we pray,
trusting in your mercy; through Jesus Christ, our Savior and Lord.
Amen.

One of the following laments may be chosen to complement the appointed biblical readings or to accompany the assembly's worship during situations of communal adversity or disaster. The lament may be part of the gathering rite, prior to the weekly intercessions, or within a devotional setting. Leaders are urged to preside with measured solemnity.

Lamenting Disease and Infirmity

With the bleeding woman of old we cry out:
Our life's blood is seeping out.
Our bones are weak, and our hearts falter.
O God, can we survive with these fragile bodies?
Some of us now, some of us later, will suffer disease.

A Kyrie or a Trisagion such as Evangelical Lutheran Worship 151–161 is sung.

Hear us, O God:
Hear us, O God.

Uphold us with your strength:
Uphold us with your strength.

Give us your life:
Give us your life.

A time of silence is kept.

Hear these words, and receive their power:
God the Father continues to create health and wholeness.
God the Son cured sick bodies and broken spirits.
God the Spirit grants us peace within our pain.

Thanks be to God:
Thanks be to God.

Lamenting Injustices in Society

With the Israelite slaves of old we cry out:
Always one group is deprived of freedoms.
The poor are forced to serve the oppressor.
O God, why are some laws so marked by unfairness?
The few have plenty to waste, although many are starving.

A Kyrie or a Trisagion such as Evangelical Lutheran Worship 151–161 is sung.

Hear us, O God:
Hear us, O God.

Form us by your justice:
Form us by your justice.

Give us your life:
Give us your life.

A time of silence is kept.

Hear these words, and receive their power:
God the Father promises a kingdom of justice and joy.
God the Son lived and died for the least of our sisters and brothers.
God the Spirit inspires us to build a city of peace.

Thanks be to God:
Thanks be to God.

Lamenting Damage to the Earth

With the ancient seer John we cry out:
We have visions of destructive storms and scorching heat.
We foresee animals dying, trees cut down, the sea swallowing up the land.
O God, is all this devastation our fault?
We want always more, and to get more, humans have damaged the earth.

A Kyrie or a Trisagion such as Evangelical Lutheran Worship 151–161 is sung.

Hear us, O God:
Hear us, O God.

Teach us your earth care:
Teach us your earth care.

Give us your life:
Give us your life.

A time of silence is kept.

Hear these words, and receive their power:
God the Father promises to restore the old and to create the new.
God the Son forgives our thoughtlessness and greed.
God the Spirit enlightens our way to wise coexistence on earth.

Thanks be to God:
Thanks be to God.

Lamenting the Grip of Melancholy

With Job of old we cry out:
Everywhere the innocent suffer.
Our desires and efforts achieve us little.
O God, are you good, yet do nothing to help us?
Our answers have holes, and we fall through.

A Kyrie or a Trisagion such as Evangelical Lutheran Worship 151–161 is sung.

Hear us, O God:
Hear us, O God.

Revive us with hope:
Revive us with hope.

Give us your life:
Give us your life.

A time of silence is kept.

Hear these words, and receive their power:
The majesty of God the Father undergirds all that is.
The mercy of God the Son accepts our despair.
The comfort of God the Spirit embraces us in communities of care.

Thanks be to God:
Thanks be to God.

Lamenting the Dread of Mortality

With Martha and Mary of old we cry out:
We grieve when our loved ones die.
Death attacks us; it shocks us all.
O God, where are you when death comes near?
We fear to die unprepared, and we dread the end of self.

A Kyrie or a Trisagion such as Evangelical Lutheran Worship 151–161 is sung.

Hear us, O God:
Hear us, O God.

Console us with your presence:
Console us with your presence.

Give us your life:
Give us your life.

A time of silence is kept.

Hear these words, and receive their power:
God the Father formed us as creatures who live and love and die.
God the Son lived a human life and joined us in death.
God the Spirit holds us in the eternal body of Christ.

Thanks be to God:
Thanks be to God.

Lamenting the Weight of Guilt

With King David of old we cry out:
Each day we hurt one another.
Each day we diminish our very selves.
O God, why are we humans so prone to evil?
My sin is my fault, my fault, my own most grievous fault.

A Kyrie or a Trisagion such as Evangelical Lutheran Worship 151–161 is sung.

Hear us, O God:
Hear us, O God.

Deliver us from our offenses:
Deliver us from our offenses.

Give us your life:
Give us your life.

A time of silence is kept.

Hear these words, and receive their power:
God the Father forgives even those sins of which we are unaware.
God the Son accompanies us in a journey toward love and obedience.
God the Spirit reconciles us to a family of forgiveness.

Thanks be to God:
Thanks be to God.

thanksgiving at the font

Praises at the Font: An Introduction

When we gather around the font, we praise God for the gift of baptismal water that washes us into life in the community of the triune God. In baptism, it is as if we join with all those whom God has saved through water—Noah in his ark, the Israelites escaping through the sea—and we remember all the biblical stories that connect Jesus himself with water.

As we thank God for baptism, we also praise God for all water. For centuries, theologians have taught that when Jesus was baptized, all the waters of the earth were consecrated. It is not that we must sanctify the water in the font; rather, we offer praises for the holiness of the water that the triune God creates and provides for this blue planet. When thanking God for water, you are encouraged to include the names of your local waters, lakes, and rivers in praise.

Such thanksgivings at the font may take place in the gathering rite of the Sunday liturgy, within the rite of holy baptism, as introduction to any affirmation of baptism, and as complement to scriptural readings that proclaim God's gift of water. Throughout our life of worship, we are singing and dancing with Miriam and the women, for evil is drowned in the waters of baptism.

Water! Water!

Water! Water! We praise you, O God, for water—
the   *local bodies of water* ,
the rain that nourishes animals and plants,
the water for drinking and bathing.
We praise you, O God, for water:
We praise you, O God, for water.

We praise you, O God, for our water stories—
a flood that cleansed the earth,
the sea that drowned the enemy,
a river that healed leprosy.
We praise you, O God, for water:
We praise you, O God, for water.

We remember the waters of Jesus—
baptized in the Jordan River,
calming the Sea of Galilee,
drinking from Jacob's Well,
healing at the pool of Bethesda,
washing the disciples' feet.
We praise you, O God, for water:
We praise you, O God, for water.

Use this paragraph at a baptism:

We praise you, O God, for this font.
Breathe into this water,
wash away the sin of all the baptized,
and birth   *name/s*   anew into your peace and joy.
We praise you, O God, for baptism:
We praise you, O God, for baptism.

Use this paragraph at a thanksgiving at the font without a baptism:

We praise you, O God, for this font,
for you breathe into this water
to wash away our sin
and birth us each day into your peace and joy.
We praise you, O God, for baptism:
We praise you, O God, for baptism.

O God, you are the Ocean, sustaining this earth.
O God, you are the River, saving us from death.
O God, you are the Fountain, granting us health and well-being.
We praise you, O God, Father, Son, and Holy Spirit,
today, tomorrow, forever.
Amen, and amen:
Amen, and amen.

Thanksgiving for the Waters of Baptism

We bless you, almighty God, for the gift of water—
for the oceans that surround the earth,
for the rivers that nurture the land,
for ___*local bodies of water*___ that you provide for our community—
we bless you, O God, for the waters of earth:
We bless you, O God, for the waters of earth.

We honor you, merciful God, for showering us with water—
for the rain that nourishes the plants and trees,
for the floods that restore the fields,
for the dew that freshens dry places—
we honor you, O God, for the waters you send:
We honor you, O God, for the waters you send.

We glorify you, gracious God, for the waters of baptism—
for the water of the Jordan that washed our Lord Jesus,
for the water that baptized the believers on Pentecost,
for the water that illumines us with your Word,
for the water that pours out the gifts of the Spirit,
for the water that bathes the church universal—the Orthodox, Roman Catholics,
    Protestants, Pentecostals, Evangelicals, independents—
we glorify you, O God, for the waters of baptism:
We glorify you, O God, for the waters of baptism.

We worship you, O God, Father, Son, and Holy Spirit,
almighty, merciful, and gracious.
Well of forgiveness, you revive us,
Cup of cold water, you refresh us,
Pool of rebirth, you renew us.
To you comes the worship of all your people, now and forever:
To you comes the worship of all your people, now and forever.

Amen.
Amen.

Thanksgiving at the Font in a Time of Flood or Drought

We gather at this font, O God,
creator of oceans and rivers, rain and snow.
We praise you for ___*local bodies of water*___ ,
and for the water you provide us each day.

We praise your Spirit, hovering over this font.
We bless you for this cleansing water of rebirth,
this flood of endless mercy,
and for all the baptized around this blue planet.

Use this paragraph in time of flood:

All the waters are yours, O God,
even the ferocious waves of the sea, the overflowing rivers,
the rainstorms that drown crops and herds.
We beg you to heed the cries
of everyone suffering from flood in ___*location*___ .
As you saved Noah and the animals from the deluge,
so now save those whose lives and livelihoods are threatened.
Dry up the wild waters, that the people may live.

Use this paragraph in time of drought:

All the waters are yours, O God,
even stagnant rivers, and wells nearly dry,
and lakes that are merely puddles.
We beg you to heed the cries
of everyone suffering from drought in ___*location*___ .
As you saved Hagar and Ishmael in the desert,
so now save all those creatures dying of thirst.
Pour down rain and fill up the wells, that the people may live.

We ask you, almighty Provider,
to give us the water we need,
and we praise you for the sustenance you grant at this font.
By the water of our baptism empower us
to pour out ourselves for others
and to safeguard the waters of your earth.

To you, Father, Son, and Holy Spirit,
Sea of holiness, Spring of salvation, Cloud of mystery,
be all praise and thanksgiving,
now and forever.
Amen.
Amen.

Thanksgiving at the Font with Children

A thanksgiving such as this may be appropriate for children under the age of seven.

Gather the children around the font. Invite the children to repeat these words:

We praise you, O God, for water:
We praise you, O God, for water.

We need water to drink:
We need water to drink.

We need water to wash:
We need water to wash.

We need water to grow:
We need water to grow.

We praise you, O God, for water:
We praise you, O God, for water.

We praise you, O God, for baptism:
We praise you, O God, for baptism.

We praise you, O God, for your Spirit:
We praise you, O God, for your Spirit.

Invite the children to stretch their hands out over the font. Pour water from a pitcher over their hands into the font.

We praise you, O God, for water:
We praise you, O God, for water.

Amen, with water:
Amen, with water.

Invite the children to mark their own or one another's foreheads with water and the sign of the cross.

thanksgivings at the table

Giving Thanks at the Table: An Introduction

For Christians, the verb "to bless" involves both giving and receiving. When Jesus fed the multitude, he "blessed" God—that is, he gave thanks to God; and when Christians eat together, they "bless" their food—that is, they receive the Spirit's power alive at their meal. The holy communion is the primary meal Christians share, and it is appropriate that the prayer of thanksgiving proclaimed at this meal be worthy of our giving and receiving blessing.

In the church's early centuries, the eucharistic prayer followed a trinitarian outline. Gathering the assembly into the very life of the triune God, such prayers praised God for acting in creation and throughout history; rehearsed the story of our salvation in the life, death, and resurrection of Jesus Christ; and asked for the Spirit to make the meal and the community into the body of Christ. In the center of the prayer, the biblical narrative of Jesus' last supper with his disciples was recounted, proclaiming the past event in the present.

By the late Middle Ages in the Western church, the eucharistic prayer had evolved into the canon of the Mass, which petitioned God to accept the offering made by the priest, whose speaking the words of institution functioned as a miraculous formula to bring Christ into the eucharistic elements. The Reformation-era scholar Philipp Melanchthon admired the quite different form of the prayer used in the Eastern church, but Martin Luther advised evangelicals simply to eliminate the eucharistic prayer. The Anglican communion composed its own obligatory text for the consecration prayer, and the evangelical Church of Sweden continued using a eucharistic prayer, but most Protestant churches severely truncated or entirely deleted this prayer, in some cases retaining only the words of institution. Perhaps some Christians do not think about a prayer of thanksgiving at the eucharist, since their method of consuming the bread and wine has lost any evocation of a meal.

In our time, the eucharistic prayer—variously titled the great thanksgiving, the anaphora, the prayer of consecration, the prayer of blessing, or the thanksgiving at the table—has evolved further. The Roman Catholic Church authorized several prayers that would have bothered Luther less. Many Protestants have begun to use trinitarian prayers that give thanks at the table of communion. The thanksgivings in this collection, composed five hundred years after the Reformation by a Lutheran and published by a Lutheran press, echo the creedal tradition of the church, proclaim evangelical theology, cite a wide range of biblical images and stories, employ contemporary rhetoric, and invite the entire assembly into trinitarian praise.

Usually these prayers will be preceded by the classic opening dialogue, a prefatory praise, and the singing of "Holy, holy, holy," and will be concluded with the assembly's praying of the Lord's Prayer. The narrative of Jesus' last supper remains in the center of the prayer. The suggestion in several prayers to replace the Pauline line "on the night in which he was betrayed" with "on the night before he died" means to speak clearly of death in a culture that prefers circumlocutions. Some traditions maintain that this narrative ought to be proclaimed outside the body of the prayer, and this variation points to the continuing inquiry as to how these words are understood to function liturgically. Presiders are encouraged to proclaim the biblical narrative as best suits their tradition. The general introduction includes advice about the printing out these prayers via the accompanying CD-ROM (see page 8).

These twenty eucharistic prayers have been crafted over five decades to meet various interests and needs. Given the variety of emphases throughout liturgical worship, no one prayer needs to say everything. Ten prayers are designed for the festivals and seasons of the liturgical year. The thanksgivings inspired by Matthew, Mark, Luke, and John support the ecumenical three-year lectionary. The prayers "after" Catherine of Siena, Julian of Norwich, and Martin Luther echo the theology, rhetoric, and imagery characteristic of their work. The Earth Prayer praises God for the cosmos that science has discovered, an idyllic Eden having been replaced or at least supplemented by awareness of the eons throughout which God oversaw both life and death. A Thanksgiving in a Time of Communal Lament provides a text for use during catastrophic sorrow. The Variable Eucharistic Prayer presents three options: a short thanksgiving; a Sunday thanksgiving; and, with ten fill-ins, a festival thanksgiving.

The hope is that some of these prayers will enrich the collection of eucharistic prayers already in your practice, as your assembly gathers with vast multitudes around Jesus, who serves our meal of mercy by becoming himself our meal.

For Advent

This Advent eucharistic prayer is based on the O Antiphons. Sung in medieval monasteries December 17–23 at evening prayer before and after the Magnificat, the antiphons used Old Testament images as descriptors of Christ. The first letters of the seven Latin words—Sapientia (Wisdom), Adonai (Lord), Radix Jesse (Root of Jesse), Clavis David (Key of David), Oriens (Sunrise), Rex Gentium (King of Nations), Emmanuel (God with us)—when read backwards, spell "Ero cras," "I will be tomorrow," that is, Christ will be here December 24. The final quatrain ("Come, Lord Jesus, be our guest") can also serve as meal prayer in the home.

We praise you, living and loving God,
that you have sent your Son to this world.
Christ is your Wisdom, sweetly ordering all creation,
our Lawgiver, burning with justice,
the Branch from Jesse's tree, sprouting flowers from old roots,
the Key of David, opening our prison doors.

And let the people cry, O come and save us:
O come and save us.

We praise you, serving and saving God,
that you send your Son also to this table,
who on the night before he died took bread, and gave thanks,
broke it, and gave it to his disciples, saying:
Take and eat; this is my body, given for you.
Do this for the remembrance of me.

Again, after supper, he took the cup, gave thanks,
and gave it for all to drink, saying:
This cup is the new covenant in my blood,
shed for you and for all people for the forgiveness of sin.
Do this for the remembrance of me.

And let the people cry, O come and save us:
O come and save us.

We beg you, mighty and merciful God:
send us the Spirit of your Son.
Dwell in this food and in all who share it,
that the earth may rejoice in your presence.
In Christ, the Dawning Day, enlighten a darkened world,
reign as Sovereign to unite all peoples,

and live among us, Emmanuel,
our deepest desire now and forever.
And let the people cry, O come and save us:
O come and save us.

Even so, come, Lord Jesus, with your Father and your Spirit, to the church,
and receive our praises, now and forever. Amen:
Amen.

And let the people pray:
Come, Lord Jesus, be our guest,
and let these gifts to us be blessed.
Blest be God, who is our Bread;
may all the world be clothed and fed. Amen.

For Christmastide

This eucharistic prayer echoes Luke 2, John 1, and the psalms appointed for Christmas: 96, 97, and 98. Given the proximity of Christmas to the Northern Hemisphere's winter solstice, it also prays for the coming of spring.

We sing a new song to you, O God of our salvation,
for you have done marvelous things.
Since the beginning of time, you have spoken your Word,
and your light shines in our darkness.
Glory to you, O God:
Glory to you, O God.

The seas are thundering with praise,
the rivers are clapping their hands.
The hills ring out with gladness,
and the trees are shouting their joy.
Glory to you, O God:
Glory to you, O God.

Your Son rules in truth and justice,
victorious and merciful is he!
We praise your majesty lying in a manger,
Jesus Christ, born of Mary and lauded by angels.
Glory to you, O God:
Glory to you, O God.

On the night before he died, Jesus took bread, and gave thanks,
broke it, and gave it to his disciples, saying:
Take and eat; this is my body, given for you.
Do this for the remembrance of me.

Again, after supper, he took the cup, gave thanks,
and gave it for all to drink, saying:
This cup is the new covenant in my blood,
shed for you and for all people for the forgiveness of sin.
Do this for the remembrance of me.

Send your Spirit on us and on this meal of wonder.
In this bread, give us the body of Christ.
With this cup, reveal the grace of your risen Son.
Make known to the whole earth your steadfast love.
Glory to you, O God:
Glory to you, O God.

In these dark days, bring the dawn of your righteousness to birth.
Hold the living and the dead in your hands.
In your good time, awaken the sleeping animals,
and revive the dormant plants with your life-giving Spirit.
Glory to you, O God:
Glory to you, O God.

With trumpets and horns and harps,
with the faithful on earth and the hosts of heaven,
we sing to your splendor, Father, Son, and Holy Spirit,
God Most High, Light of the earth, and Judge of the world,
today and forever. Amen.
Amen.

For Epiphany and Transfiguration

This eucharistic prayer is based on the 1599 Epiphany hymn Wie schön leuchtet der
Morgenstern. *Honored as the Queen of Chorales and translated as "O Morning Star, how fair
and bright!" (Evangelical Lutheran Worship 308), it was written and composed by Philipp
Nicolai. The presider may chant the words printed in alternate typeface to the suggested pitches,
which echo the chorale. The remaining text can be spoken, intoned freely, or chanted using other
phrases from the hymn tune.*

Al-might-y Lord, we praise your shining light, your glowing grace.   *[do-sol-mi-do]*
From before the earth's foundation, you loved us and promised us life forever.
Within the earth's deep sadness, we laud your great and glorious might.
Despite our tears and sinning, we sing of the gladness of your mercy.

We praise your Son, our Morn-ing Star.   *[do-sol-mi-do]*
Christ is our dia-mond bright, our trea-sure dear.   *[do-sol-mi-do, sol-la-la-sol]*
He is our living Savior who has ransomed us in love.
He keeps us yours and fails us never—today, tomorrow, and every day.

On the night before his great salvation, he took bread and gave thanks,
broke it, and gave it to his disciples, saying:
Take and eat; this is my body, given for you.
Do this for the remembrance of me.

Again, after supper, he took the cup, gave thanks,
and gave it for all to drink, saying:
This cup is the new covenant in my blood,
shed for you and for all people for the forgiveness of sin.
Do this for the remembrance of me.

With joy we tell our story:
Al-le-lu-ia!   *[sol-mi-sol-mi]*
Al-le-lu-ia!   *[sol-mi-sol-mi]*

We call for your Spirit on us and this meal.
Refresh our souls with this heavenly food, the body and blood of your Son.
Nourish us as branches of your tree,
and enlighten us with your undying flame.

We sing out to the Father, we ring out to the Son, we exult in the Spirit.
Transport us in our yearning,
and be for us the end and the beginning,
our purest pleasure, our victorious crown, our never-ending love.
And so we pray and praise:
A-men, a-men, a-men, a-men.   *[high do-sol-la-so, fa-mi-re-do]*
A-men, a-men, a-men, a-men.   *[high do-sol-la-so, fa-mi-re-do]*

For Lent

O God, Creator of our wilderness world,
O God, Savior of the lost,
O God, Comforter of the sick and suffering,
we give you thanks for your everlasting might;
we glorify you for your covenant of mercy.

(Bracketed lines below are optional)
For forty days you cleansed the earth with the waters of the flood.
[We praise you, O God: **We praise you, O God.**]
For forty days you illumined Moses with the words of your law.
[We praise you, O God: **We praise you, O God.**]
For forty years you fed your people with manna from heaven.
[We praise you, O God: **We praise you, O God.**]

You became truly human in Jesus our brother.
For forty days, with fasting and prayer, he renounced the power of the devil.
On the night before he died he took bread, and gave thanks,
broke it, and gave it to his disciples, saying:
Take and eat; this is my body, given for you.
Do this for the remembrance of me.

Again, after supper, he took the cup, gave thanks,
and gave it for all to drink, saying:
This cup is the new covenant in my blood,
shed for you and for all people for the forgiveness of sin.
Do this for the remembrance of me.

We extol his life. Amen:
Amen.

We lament his death. Amen:
Amen.

We celebrate his resurrection. Amen:
Amen.

Transform us, O God, with your lively Spirit.

Make this food into manna for our journey, the body and blood of your Son.

[Save us, O God: **Save us, O God.**]

Grant us with the Ninevites forty days of repentance.

[Save us, O God: **Save us, O God.**]

Teach us your words of wisdom and justice.

[Save us, O God: **Save us, O God.**]

Renew the whole earth with baptismal grace.

[Save us, O God: **Save us, O God.**]

At the last, lead all your pilgrim people through our deserts to your Easter garden.

To you, O God, Creator, Savior, Comforter,

Father, Son, and Holy Spirit,

be our worship and praise, adoration and thanksgiving,

now and forever. Amen.

Amen.

For Maundy Thursday

This concise eucharistic prayer, echoing Jewish table blessing, is appropriate for Maundy Thursday, a lengthy service that includes individual absolution, footwashing, and communion.

Blessed are you, O living God, sovereign of time and space.
You bring forth bread from the earth and fruit from the vine.
Your word leads us across the waters to freedom,
passing over with us from death to life.
Blessed be God forever!
Blessed be God forever!

Blessed are you, O living God, for your glory revealed in Jesus Christ.
He is the Lamb, whose blood saves us from sin.
He is your Servant, who washes our feet with mercy.
He is himself our Food, the bread and cup of salvation.
Blessed be God forever!
Blessed be God forever!

On the night in which he was betrayed, he took bread, and gave thanks,
broke it, and gave it to his disciples, saying:
Take and eat; this is my body, given for you.
Do this for the remembrance of me.

Again, after supper, he took the cup, gave thanks,
and gave it for all to drink, saying:
This cup is the new covenant in my blood,
shed for you and for all people for the forgiveness of sin.
Do this for the remembrance of me.

Blessed be God forever!
Blessed be God forever!

Blessed are you, O living God, for your Spirit of love.
Feed us at this table with the body and blood of your Son.
Make us servants of one another and of everyone in need.
Bring us with all your people to the joy of the resurrection.
Blessed be God forever!
Blessed be God forever!

Amen, Amen.
Amen, Amen.

For the Resurrection of Our Lord: Easter Day

This eucharistic prayer for Easter Day echoes the Easter proclamation that was chanted at the Vigil of Easter.

This is the day that in joy and delight
we join with all the angels of heaven and all the creatures on earth
to sing our praise and thanksgiving to you,
all holy and mighty and glorious God.
For Christ is risen:
Christ is risen indeed.

This is the day that you gave light to the earth.
This is the day that you saved the Israelites through the sea
and with your pillar of fire led them to freedom.
Now every night is as bright as day,
and that light is Christ:
Thanks be to God.

This is the day that you broke the chains of death.
This is the day that, marrying heaven to earth,
you washed away sin, rescued us from evil, and brought us your peace.
The Lamb who was slain has begun to reign,
for Christ is risen:
Christ is risen indeed.

On the night before he died, our Lord Jesus Christ took bread, and gave thanks,
broke it, and gave it to his disciples, saying:
Take and eat; this is my body, given for you.
Do this for the remembrance of me.

Again, after supper, he took the cup, gave thanks,
and gave it for all to drink, saying:
This cup is the new covenant in my blood,
shed for you and for all people for the forgiveness of sin.
Do this for the remembrance of me.

Let us proclaim the mystery of faith:
Christ has died. Christ is risen. Christ will come again.

On this day send us the power of your Holy Spirit.
Revive us with the body and blood of our risen Savior.
Illumine our lives with your presence,
and shine your Morning Star over the whole human race,
for that light is Christ:
Thanks be to God.

All holy and mighty and glorious God,
radiant Father, victorious Son, and shining Spirit,
we bless your salvation, we sing of your mercy,
and we praise your victory through all time and space,
for Christ is risen:
Christ is risen indeed.

Amen and amen:
Amen and amen.

For Pentecost and Spirit Festivals

Thanks be to you, O God, for the power of your loving Spirit.
We worship you for your Spirit, who forms life out of chaos and dust.
We bless you for your Spirit, who ignites the words of the prophets.
We praise you for your Spirit, who carries your people together in unity.

Glory be to you, O God, for the comfort of your creative Spirit.
By your Spirit your Son preached and healed, rebuked and forgave.
Dying on the cross for a wounded world, he gave over his Spirit.
Risen from death, he pours out your Spirit on all who believe.

On the night before he died, our Lord Jesus took bread, and gave thanks,
broke it, and gave it to his disciples, saying:
Take and eat; this is my body, given for you.
Do this for the remembrance of me.

Again, after supper, he took the cup, gave thanks,
and gave it for all to drink, saying:
This cup is the new covenant in my blood,
shed for you and for all people for the forgiveness of sin.
Do this for the remembrance of me.

On this bread and wine, come, Holy Spirit:
Come, Holy Spirit.

Manifest here the body and blood of Christ. Come, Holy Spirit:
Come, Holy Spirit.

On this assembly, come, Holy Spirit:
Come, Holy Spirit.

On baptismal festivals, add:

On ___name/s___ and on all the newly baptized, come, Holy Spirit:
Come, Holy Spirit.

On a day of confirmation, add:

On the members of this confirmation class, come, Holy Spirit:
Come, Holy Spirit.

At installations, ordinations, and consecrations, add:

On ___name/s___ , come, Holy Spirit:
Come, Holy Spirit.

At church conventions, add:

On all who minister in your church, come, Holy Spirit:
Come, Holy Spirit.

On this earth, its waters and lands and skies, come, Holy Spirit:
Come, Holy Spirit.

On plants and animals, and even on the stars, come, Holy Spirit:
Come, Holy Spirit.

We plead for your Spirit, to cry aloud in us, with us, and for us.
Breathe your life into our bones.
Anoint us for service with your oil of gladness.
Translate our speech into tongues of wisdom.
Shower on us your gifts:
   love, joy, peace, patience, kindness,
   generosity, faithfulness, gentleness, self-control.
Sanctify the whole earth with your truth.
Bring us at the end with all your needy children into your homeland of mercy.

Once more we praise and worship and bless you,
Father, Son, and Holy Spirit,
God of supreme mercy and might,
God of the cross and the empty tomb,
God of the power of justice and peace,
now and forever.
Amen.
Amen.

For Trinity Sunday: Triple Praise

This expansive Triple Praise is appropriate for Trinity Sunday and for other high festivals. Note that as formatted, the first section replaces the proper preface.

Holy God, Holy One, Holy Three!
Before all that is, you were God.
  Outside all we know, you are God.
    After all is finished, you will be God.
Archangels sound the trumpets,
  Angels teach us their song,
    Saints pull us into your presence.

And this is our song:
Holy, holy, holy . . .

Holy God, Holy One, Holy Three!
You beyond the galaxies,
  You under the oceans,
    You inside the leaves,
You pouring down rain,
  You opening the flowers,
    You feeding the insects,
You giving us your image,
  You carrying us through the waters,
    You holding us in the night;
Your smile on Sarah and Abraham,
  Your hand with Moses and Miriam,
    Your words through Deborah and Isaiah,
You lived as Jesus among us,
  Healing, teaching, dying, rising,
    Inviting us all to your feast.

In the night in which he was betrayed he took bread, and gave thanks,
broke it, and gave it to his disciples, saying:
Take and eat; this is my body, given for you.
Do this for the remembrance of me.

Again, after supper, he took the cup, gave thanks,
and gave it for all to drink, saying:
This cup is the new covenant in my blood,
shed for you and for all people for the forgiveness of sin.
Do this for the remembrance of me.

Holy God, we remember your Son,
His life with the humble,
   His death among the wretched,
      His resurrection for us all:
Your wisdom our guide,
   Your justice our strength,
      Your grace our path to rebirth.

And so we cry, Mercy:
Mercy!

And so we cry, Glory:
Glory!

And so we cry, Blessing:
Blessing!

Holy God, we beg for your Spirit:
Enliven this bread,
   Awaken this body,
      Pour us out for each other.
Transfigure our minds,
   Ignite your church,
      Nourish the life of the earth.
Make us, while many, united,
   Make us, though broken, whole,
      Make us, despite death, alive.

And so we cry, Come, Holy Spirit:
Come, Holy Spirit!

And so the church shouts, Come, Holy Spirit:
Come, Holy Spirit!

And so the earth pleads, Come, Holy Spirit:
Come, Holy Spirit!

You, Holy God, Holy One, Holy Three,
Our Life, our Mercy, our Might,
  Our Table, our Food, our Server,
    Our Rainbow, our Ark, our Dove,
Our Sovereign, our Water, our Wine,
  Our Light, our Treasure, our Tree,
    Our Way, our Truth, our Life.
You, Holy God, Holy One, Holy Three!
Praise now,
  Praise tomorrow,
    Praise forever.

And so we cry, Amen, amen:
Amen, amen!

For All Saints

This All Saints eucharistic prayer is appropriate also during the Week of Prayer for Christian Unity and for select funerals.

With all the saints
    of Africa and Asia, Europe and the Americas, India, Australia, and the islands,
    we praise you, O God, for creating the worlds.
With all the baptized,
    the old and the young, the weak and the strong, the famous and the forgotten,
    we bless you, O God, for providing mortals with food.
With all the faithful
    in tents and mansions, cities and farms, past and present,
    we worship you, O God, for sheltering the generations.
With all your holy people
    who minister in the church, who serve the poor, who walk the way of the cross,
    we glorify you, O God, for journeying with us in Jesus.

With Paul and the evangelists,
    we remember the meal of your Son:
On the night before he died, he took bread, and gave thanks,
broke it, and gave it to his disciples, saying:
Take and eat; this is my body, given for you.
Do this for the remembrance of me.

Again, after supper, he took the cup, gave thanks,
and gave it for all to drink, saying:
This cup is the new covenant in my blood,
shed for you and for all people for the forgiveness of sin.
Do this for the remembrance of me.

With Peter and all the martyrs,
    we honor Christ's death, saying Amen.
Amen!

With Mary Magdalene and all the apostles,
    we proclaim his resurrection, shouting Amen.
Amen!

With John, the theologians, and the mystics,
    we celebrate Christ present with us, exclaiming Amen.
Amen!

With the Virgin Mary and all who sang of your greatness,
    we pray for the power of the Spirit.
    Imbue this gathering, this bread and this cup,
    with the merciful body and blood of Christ.
    Form us into a communion of service,
    and infuse your earth with the wholeness we seek.

With grandparents and godparents,
    with the Orthodox, Roman Catholics, Protestants, Pentecostals, Evangelicals,
      and independents,
    and with   *name/s of beloved saints or the local deceased* ,
    lead us to a future we cannot yet see,
    and at the end draw all humanity to yourself.

Now with all of the family you saved by your love,
    we shout blessing: **Blessing**
    glory: **Glory**
    wisdom: **Wisdom**
    thanksgiving: **Thanksgiving**
    honor: **Honor**
    power: **Power**
    might: **Might**
    be to you, our God, forever and ever.
Amen.
Amen.

For the Reign of Christ the King

This eucharistic prayer applies the metaphor of sovereignty to all three persons of the Trinity.

We bless you, O God, Sovereign of all things, Might of the ages.
We your people praise your mystery, ever one, always three.

O radiant Source of creation, you brought light out of darkness.
Planets and stars, plants and animals receive their life from your throne.
Apostles, monarchs, parents, children: your dominion enlivens us all.
We praise your majestic power, saying,
Blessing and glory to you, O God:
Blessing and glory to you, O God.

O Christ Jesus, Ruler and Guide, you call us to follow your path.
Your scepter is your hand reaching out to the needy.
We bow before you, enthroned on the cross.
We laud your supreme mercy, saying,
Wisdom and thanks to you, O God:
Wisdom and thanks to you, O God.

On the night before he died, our Lord Jesus Christ took bread, and gave thanks,
broke it, and gave it to his disciples, saying:
Take and eat; this is my body, given for you.
Do this for the remembrance of me.

Again, after supper, he took the cup, gave thanks,
and gave it for all to drink, saying:
This cup is the new covenant in my blood,
shed for you and for all people for the forgiveness of sin.
Do this for the remembrance of me.

We remember his life of service,
his suffering and death, and his rising to eternal life.
We acclaim the reign of Christ our King, saying,
Honor to you, O God:
Honor to you, O God.

O Spirit, our supreme Defender, transform this meal into the banquet of life.
Gather all the sick and the poor into your palace of safekeeping.
Govern the nations with your justice and peace.
We plead for your surpassing grace, saying,
Power and might to you, O God:
Power and might to you, O God.

O God the Father, you uphold the universe that you create;
O God the Son, you are crowned with compassion for all;
O God the Spirit, you protect your saints with arms of love.
We praise you today, tomorrow, and forever. Amen.
Amen.

Once more:
Amen.

And once more:
Amen.

A Eucharistic Prayer Inspired by Matthew

This eucharistic prayer, appropriate for year A of the lectionary and for the commemoration of St. Matthew, September 21, echoes the content of Matthew's gospel and its attention to the Jewish roots of Christianity.

Blessed are you, Lord of heaven and earth.
From age to age your creation sings your praises.
You feed even the birds of the air,
and you clothe the fields with lilies.
You gave your blessing to Abraham and his descendants,
and you spoke with Moses, Elijah, and David.
Blessed are you, Lord our God:
Blessed are you, Lord our God.

You fulfilled your covenant with us in Jesus.
He is Emmanuel, your beloved Son,
the star that guides us to wisdom,
the treasure hidden in a field.
He is the landowner who overpays the workers,
the judge who separates good from evil.
Blessed are you, Lord our God:
Blessed are you, Lord our God.

For us he lived, for us he died, for us he rose to eternal life.
Then and now he invites us to your banquet.
On the night in which he was betrayed, he took bread, and gave thanks,
broke it, and gave it to his disciples, saying:
Take and eat; this is my body, given for you.
Do this for the remembrance of me.

Again, after supper, he took the cup, gave thanks,
and gave it for all to drink, saying:
This cup is the new covenant in my blood,
shed for you and for all people for the forgiveness of sin.
Do this for the remembrance of me.

We hear his call, we repent our ways,
and we enter with joy into the kingdom of heaven.
Blessed are you, Lord our God:
Blessed are you, Lord our God.

Send your Holy Spirit here on your gathered disciples.
Make of this meal the body and blood of forgiveness.
Heal us and grant us your righteousness,
that we may love you and serve our neighbors.
Blessed are you, Lord our God:
Blessed are you, Lord our God.

Blessed are you, Lord our God,
our Father in heaven,
the Rock on which we build,
the Dove alighting on us all.
We worship you and sing our praises,
today and to the end of the age.
Amen.
Amen.

A Eucharistic Prayer Inspired by Mark

This eucharistic prayer, appropriate for year B of the lectionary and for the commemoration of St. Mark, April 25, echoes the themes of this earliest gospel.

Blessed are you, Lord our God,
for creating us to live together in unity
and for forgiving our failures in following your call.
Blessed are you, Abba Father,
for sending your beloved Son
and for adopting us to be your family of sisters and brothers.
Lord, we receive this good news:
Lord, we receive this good news.

Blessed are you, Sovereign of mercy,
for establishing your kingdom in Jesus the Messiah.
He healed the sick, and welcomed women and men, and taught the
    commandments.
Blessed is he, the Son of Man, who became a servant of all,
and who overcomes the might of Satan until the end of time.
Lord, we believe this good news:
Lord, we believe this good news.

On the night in which he was betrayed, he took bread, and gave thanks,
broke it, and gave it to his disciples, saying:
Take and eat; this is my body, given for you.
Do this for the remembrance of me.

Again, after supper, he took the cup, gave thanks,
and gave it for all to drink, saying:
This cup is the new covenant in my blood,
shed for you and for all people for the forgiveness of sin.
Do this for the remembrance of me.

We remember the good news of his life given for us,
his death on the cross, and his rising from the tomb, and together we say,
Christ has died. Christ is risen. Christ will come again.
Christ has died. Christ is risen. Christ will come again.

By the power of your Spirit, hidden in the ministry of Jesus,
reveal yourself to us here, hidden in this bread and cup.
Do not forsake us, but save us in the time of trial.
By this mystery of Christ's body and blood, cast out our demons,
cleanse our hearts, and strengthen our service toward all in need.
Lord, do not ever forsake us:
Lord, do not ever forsake us.

To you, Lord God, the Blessed One,
and to your Son, coming at the end in glory,
and to the Holy Spirit, descending on us now like a dove,
be all our praise and thanksgiving, now and forever.
Amen.
Amen.

A Eucharistic Prayer Inspired by Luke

This eucharistic prayer, appropriate for year C of the lectionary and for the commemoration of St. Luke, October 18, echoes the content of Luke's gospel and the Acts of the Apostles and their witness to the power of the Holy Spirit.

Blessed are you, God Most High!
We give thanks for your holy covenant,
your promise to Abraham,
your mercy to the house of David,
your word spoken through the prophets,
and your beloved Son, the dawn of our salvation.
We praise and magnify you, O God!
We praise and magnify you, O God!

Blessed are you, Jesus Christ, forgiving Savior, merciful Lord.
We trust in your tender compassion.
You are the good Samaritan, we the wounded traveler.
You are the sweeping woman, we the lost coin.
You ate with Mary, Martha, and Zacchaeus,
and you filled Emmaus with your resurrection.
We praise and magnify you, O God!
We praise and magnify you, O God!

On the night in which our Lord Jesus Christ was betrayed,
he took bread, and gave thanks,
broke it, and gave it to his disciples, saying:
Take and eat; this is my body, given for you.
Do this for the remembrance of me.

Again, after supper, he took the cup, gave thanks,
and gave it for all to drink, saying:
This cup is the new covenant in my blood,
shed for you and for all people for the forgiveness of sin.
Do this for the remembrance of me.

For this meal and for your presence within it, we sing:
We praise and magnify you, O God!
We praise and magnify you, O God!

Blessed are you, Holy Spirit, Power of the Most High.
As you came to Mary, come to us and to this meal.
Welcome us home, that together we may feast on your love.
Feed us with the body of Christ, that we may be holy and righteous before you.
Heal us, that with Dorcas we may rise to serve those in need.
Send us into all the world, preaching the power of your peace.
We praise and magnify you, O God!
We praise and magnify you, O God!

Blessed are you, Mighty One, Father, Son, and Spirit,
Shepherd of forgiveness, Author of life, Light in our darkness.
We join with the multitude of angels to praise and magnify your name,
singing, Glory to God in the highest heaven,
today, tomorrow, and forever.
Amen.
Amen.

A Eucharistic Prayer inspired by John

This eucharistic prayer, appropriate for the commemoration of John, December 27, and for whenever the Gospel according to John is proclaimed, echoes the theology and narratives of the fourth gospel.

Glory to you, God from before the beginning,
God bearing from above your Word of grace,
God sending on us the Dove of peace.
Glory to you, O God!
Glory to you, O God!

You are the great I AM,
feeding your people with manna in the wilderness.
You are the Father of our beloved Jesus,
whom you gave to the world
to be the Lamb, the King of Israel, the Son of Man.
Glory to you, O God!
Glory to you, O God!

You anointed Jesus to be our messiah and teacher.
He is the bread from heaven, the fruitful vine,
the good shepherd, the gate of protection, our very Lord and God,
our way, our truth, and our resurrection to life eternal.
Glory to you, O God!
Glory to you, O God!

On the night that he washed his disciples' feet,
he took bread, and gave thanks,
broke it, and gave it to his disciples, saying:
Take and eat; this is my body, given for you.
Do this for the remembrance of me.

Again, after supper, he took the cup, gave thanks,
and gave it for all to drink, saying:
This cup is the new covenant in my blood,
shed for you and for all people for the forgiveness of sin.
Do this for the remembrance of me.

With Lazarus we wait in our tomb,
we hear you call our name,
and we come out from our death into your life.
With Mary Magdalene we cry out,
We have seen the Lord.
We have seen the Lord.

(or stanza 1 of "We have seen the Lord," ELW 869)

Breathe your Spirit of power on us.
Nourish us with your living water,
and sustain us with the body and blood of your Son.
Claim us as your friends.
Birth us anew and enlighten our eyes.
Unbind us, that as your servants we may unbind one another.
Glory to you, O God!
Glory to you, O God!

Glory to you, O God, Father, Son, and Holy Spirit,
the Source of all, the Light of the world, the Advocate for your children.

Blessing: **Blessing**
and thanksgiving: **Thanksgiving**
and honor: **Honor**
and might: **Might**
be to you forever and ever.
Amen.
Amen.

A Eucharistic Prayer after Catherine of Siena

This eucharistic prayer, representing the church's mystical tradition, is composed from the ecstatic meditations of Catherine of Siena, especially numbers 10 and 17. The prayer is appropriate for devotional retreats and for the commemoration of Catherine of Siena, April 29.

O eternal Trinity!
O fire and deep well of charity!
O you who are madly in love with your creature!
O eternal truth!
O eternal fire!
O eternal wisdom, given for our redemption!
In your light we have seen light.
Your wonderful works are known
because they come forth from you who is light.

We are trees of death, but you are the tree of life.
When you saw that our tree could bear no fruit,
you came to its rescue
with the same love with which you had created it.
You engrafted your divinity into the dead tree of our humanity.
O sweet tender engrafting!

Not only did you gift us with creation in your image and likeness,
but you created us anew in grace in your Son's blood,
and you give us yourself, love immeasurable.
You, eternal Father, are the table
that offers us as food the Lamb.
Your Son is the most exquisite of foods for us,
nourishing us in your will
and strengthening us pilgrim travelers in this life.
And the Holy Spirit is indeed a waiter for us,
serving us the teaching of charity for our neighbors.

On the night before he died, our Lord Jesus Christ took bread, and gave thanks,
broke it, and gave it to his disciples, saying:
Take and eat; this is my body, given for you.
Do this for the remembrance of me.

Again, after supper, he took the cup, gave thanks,
and gave it for all to drink, saying:
This cup is the new covenant in my blood,
shed for you and for all people for the forgiveness of sin.
Do this for the remembrance of me.

By making yourself small, you have made us great.
By stripping yourself of life, you have clothed us in grace.
By being stretched out on the cross, you have embraced us.
For us you have made a cavern in your open side,
where we find refuge.

Together we proclaim:
We proclaim the power of the eternal God,
We proclaim the wisdom of the Son,
We proclaim the mercy of the Holy Spirit.

Power of the eternal Father, help us!
Wisdom of the Son, enlighten the eye of our understanding!
Tender mercy of the Holy Spirit,
enflame our hearts and unite them to yourself.
Set our hearts ablaze with your fire,
with desire to love and follow you in truth.

Within us is eternal life, and we do not know it!
Eternal God,
restore health to the sick and life to the dead.
Give us a voice, your own voice,
to cry out to you for mercy for the world
and for the reform of holy church.

O eternal Trinity, our sweet love!
You, light, give us light!
You, wisdom, give us wisdom!
You, supreme strength, give us strength!
O eternal Trinity!
O fire and deep well of charity!
O you who are madly in love with your creatures!
O eternal truth!
O eternal fire!
O eternal wisdom, given for our redemption!

Grant us your gentle and eternal benediction.
Amen.
Amen.

A Eucharistic Prayer after Julian of Norwich

This eucharistic prayer, inspired by Julian of Norwich's Revelations of Divine Love, is appropriate for the second Sunday of Lent in year A, for the commemoration of Julian, May 8, and whenever the imagery of the divine mother is sought.

Thanks be to you, our God, blessed Trinity.
You are all-mighty, all-wisdom, all-truth.

In you, our Maker, is our endless bliss.
You hold the universe tenderly,
for you love everything you have made.
You long for us to be one with you,
beholding us as your children, innocent and lovable,
and in your gracious goodness you desire that all shall be well:
All shall be well.

And when we had fallen, Jesus fell with us, embracing us,
assuring us that at the end, all shall be well:
All shall be well.

In plenteous love, Jesus donned the soiled tunic of Adam
and, becoming our Clothing, dressed us in himself,
wrapping us round in compassion.
Jesus is our dear Mother,
whose marvelous mercy is nearest, and readiest, and surest.
In his sorrowful passion, Jesus suffered to bear us into life.
Indeed, we laugh mightily, for the fiend is overcome.
Jesus mothers us, washing us clean and cleaving to us,
keeping us safe and secure.
He poured out his precious blood from his open side,
that he might nurse us with the sweet milk of himself.
He wears us now as his crown,
for immeasurable love is his meaning and delight.

In the night before he bled out his life for us,
he took bread, and gave thanks,
broke it, and gave it to his disciples, saying:
Take and eat; this is my body, given for you.
Do this for the remembrance of me.

Again, after supper, he took the cup, gave thanks,
and gave it for all to drink, saying:
This cup is the new covenant in my blood,
shed for you and for all people for the forgiveness of sin.
Do this for the remembrance of me.

Show us here the surpassing kindness of the Spirit, our Keeper.
In this blessed sacrament of abundant love,
sustain us with the body and blood of true life.
We your children beseech you
to keep us in everlasting fullness of joy.
By the tender touch and gracious working of your care,
protect and comfort us, nourish and teach us,
and unite us with you and to one another.

Until the whole communion of saints is lovingly hidden in you,
we join in hope, in praise and thanksgiving, that in you
All shall be well, and all shall be well, and all manner of things shall be well:
All shall be well, and all shall be well, and all manner of things shall be well.

To you, O God, blessed Trinity,
who is Truth, Wisdom, and Love,
Friend and Spouse, Nurse and Leader, Light and Sovereign,
our Ground and our Heaven,
be endless thanksgiving for your merciful goodness,
for you are our bliss, now and forever.
Amen.
Amen.

A Eucharistic Prayer after Martin Luther

Martin Luther denounced the theology of the medieval Roman canon and did not himself compose a full evangelical eucharistic prayer. However, we can create a thanksgiving at the table using phrases from his hymns. Within the ELCA and ELCIC, this eucharistic prayer is appropriate for the commemoration of Martin Luther, February 18 (if during Lent, either omit the "Hallelujah" or substitute "Lord, have mercy."); the Presentation of the Augsburg Confession and the commemoration of Philipp Melanchthon, June 25; Reformation Day, October 31; the commemoration of Katharina von Bora Luther, December 20; and for occasional services that celebrate Lutheran identity. The Hallelujah can be shouted or sung.

Lord God, we praise you, bless you, and adore you.
In thanksgiving we bow before you.
O loving Father! You have created all,
and you care for your children day and night.
Hallelujah!
Hallelujah!

You sent your Son to bring us your salvation.
Christ is the source of every grace and blessing,
the true paschal lamb and bread of heaven,
the very joy of all, the sun that warms and lights us.
Hallelujah!
Hallelujah!

On the night in which he was betrayed, he took bread, and gave thanks,
broke it, and gave it to his disciples, saying:
Take and eat; this is my body, given for you.
Do this for the remembrance of me.

Again, after supper, he took the cup, gave thanks,
and gave it for all to drink, saying:
This cup is the new covenant in my blood,
shed for you and for all people for the forgiveness of sin.
Do this for the remembrance of me.

We remember Jesus, your Word made flesh, our elder brother,
dying on the accursed tree,
crushing the power of hell,
and rising again victorious from the grave.
Hallelujah!
Hallelujah!

Send your Spirit on this holy feast.
Nourish and heal us with the body and blood of our Savior.
Bestow on your church your sweetest love,
your transcendent comfort, your unity and peace.
Hallelujah!
Hallelujah!

To you, the one true God,
Father, Son, and Holy Spirit,
we give our thanks and praise,
joining now and forever in loud songs of
Hallelujah!
Hallelujah!

Amen.
Amen.

An Earth Eucharistic Prayer

Much Christian praise evokes the ancient belief that God created earth as a paradise in which death was contrary to the divine will. In response to centuries of scientific discovery, this Earth Eucharistic Prayer confesses a God who created a world in which from its beginnings life contends with death. Thus Christ's death and resurrection do not deny God's natural order, but rather epitomize and sanctify it. The refrain can be sung simply, the first time on the note sol, the second time on la, the third time on ti, and lastly on do.

O God triune, how majestic is your name in all the earth.
Over the eons your merciful might evolved our home, a fragile tree of life.
Here by your wisdom are both life and death, growth and decay,
the nest and the hunt, sunshine and storm.
Sustained by these wonders, we creatures of dust join in the ancient song:
The earth is full of your glory:
The earth is full of your glory.

O God triune, you took on our flesh in Jesus our healer.
In Christ you bring life from death; we remember his cross, we laud his
    resurrection.
Broken like bread, he enlivens our body.
Outpoured like wine, he fills the earth with goodness.
Receiving this mystery, we mortals sing our song:
The earth is full of your glory:
The earth is full of your glory.

We praise you for the heart of Jesus,
so filled with your love for this earth.

On the night before he died, he took bread, and gave thanks,
broke it, and gave it to his disciples, saying:
Take and eat; this is my body, given for you.
Do this for the remembrance of me.

Again, after supper, he took the cup, gave thanks,
and gave it for all to drink, saying:
This cup is the new covenant in my blood,
shed for you and for all people for the forgiveness of sin.
Do this for the remembrance of me.

Gathered around this table, we your children unite in this song:
The earth is full of your glory:
The earth is full of your glory.

O God triune, you create the worlds, you uphold the living, you embrace the dead.
Send forth your Spirit and renew the face of the earth.
Strengthen us for our journey with this meal, the body and blood of Christ.
Give us a future that trusts in you and cares for your earth.
Empowered by your promises, we rise from our deaths to praise you again:
The earth is full of your glory:
The earth is full of your glory.

Amen, and Amen.
Amen, and Amen.

Thanksgiving in a Time of Communal Lament

This eucharistic prayer, combining lament and thanksgiving, is designed for a time of extreme communal suffering.

God of infinite mystery, God of everlasting promise,
we gather at this table in sorrow.
We have been met with disaster,
and we grieve for all who suffer.
God our fortress, God our shield, God our healer,
receive our lament,
and listen to our silent prayers.
(Keep silence for a time.)
Weep with us, merciful God:
Weep with us, merciful God.

And yet God of endless compassion, God of eternal mercy,
always we gather at this table in thanksgiving.
Your majestic creation knew conflict from its very beginnings,
yet in all things you overcome death with life.
God our homeland, God our guardian, God our nurse,
you freed the slaves, you vanquished the enemy,
you fed the starving, you cured the sick,
and you filled the sky with the rainbow of hope.
Rescue us, mighty God:
Rescue us, mighty God.

We give you thanks for your Son,
who himself knew evil and pain.
He wept over the city, he mourned the death of his friend,
yet he sought healing for the whole world.

On the night before he died, our Lord Jesus took bread and gave thanks,
broke it, and gave it to his disciples, saying:
Take and eat; this is my body, given for you.
Do this for the remembrance of me.

Again, after supper, he took the cup, gave thanks,
and gave it for all to drink, saying:
This cup is the new covenant in my blood,
shed for you and for all people for the forgiveness of sin.
Do this for the remembrance of me.

We remember his life with the poor and his death with the outcast,
and we rejoice in his resurrection,
which promises the world release from agony and destruction.
Remember us, faithful God:
Remember us, faithful God.

Make this meal into your body and blood of forgiveness.
Strengthen us to wait in faith for your peace and justice, health and joy,
until that day when your creation is born anew
to live without heartache and affliction.
Preserve us, compassionate God:
Preserve us, compassionate God.

To you, God of ceaseless consolation, God of unending goodness,
Father, Son, and Holy Spirit,
we offer here our laments and our thanksgivings,
for your hands hold our tears
and your ears receive our praises,
now and forever.
Amen.
Amen.

A Variable Eucharistic Prayer

This Variable Eucharistic Prayer offers three options. For a concise eucharistic prayer in pastoral care situations, use the lines marked A. For Sunday worship, use the lines marked A and B. For festivals, fill in the lines marked C with phrases appropriate to the occasion and the biblical readings of the day, and use the lines marked A, B, and C.

A   We praise you, all-holy God,

B   our maker, our lover, our keeper,

C   _descriptors of God appropriate to the occasion or biblical readings_   ,

A   for the universe beyond our knowing,

B   for lands and seas and all their animals,

C   for   _local natural life_   ,

A   and for friends and strangers and family,

B   for homes and grocery stores and schools,

C   for   _several significant local places_   .

A   We praise you for your covenant people,

B   for Abraham and Sarah, Moses and Miriam,

C   for   _more Old Testament figures_   ,

A   and for centuries of faithful Christians,

B   for Mary and Mary Magdalene, Peter and Paul,

C   and for   _more beloved saints_   .

A   We praise you for your Son Jesus Christ,

B   who saves us from sin and from evil,

C   who   _an aspect of his ministry appropriate to the occasion or biblical readings_   ,

A   who on the night before he died took bread, and gave thanks,
broke it, and gave it to his disciples, saying:
Take and eat; this is my body, given for you.
Do this for the remembrance of me.

Again, after supper, he took the cup, gave thanks,
and gave it for all to drink, saying:
This cup is the new covenant in my blood,
shed for you and for all people for the forgiveness of sin.
Do this for the remembrance of me.

A   And so we proclaim the mystery of our faith:

A   **Christ has died. Christ is risen. Christ will come again.**

A   We pray for your Holy Spirit,

B   your breath, your fire, your wisdom,

C   <u>*an action of the Spirit appropriate to the occasion or biblical readings*</u> .

A   Nourish us with the body and blood of Christ,

B   inspire your people for service,

C   <u>*a plea with local interest*</u> ,

A   and renew the world with your mercy,

B   with your healing, your justice, and your peace,

C   that <u>*reference to the occasion or biblical readings*</u> .

A   We praise you, all-holy God,

B   the Father, the Son, the Holy Spirit,

C   <u>*three Trinitarian images appropriate to the occasion or biblical readings*</u> ,

A   today, tomorrow, and forever. Amen!

A   Amen!

Image Credits

The cover art reproduces the familiar image of the Veiled Orante, the woman praying in the orans posture, painted in the late second century on the wall of a cubiculum in the Roman Catacomb of Priscilla. She is flanked with scenes of her marriage and her motherhood. On the ceiling of this small tomb room is a painting of Christ the good shepherd, and on the walls are the sacrifice of Isaac, Jonah and the sea monster, and the three men in the fiery furnace—three Easter Vigil readings. Image copyright © REUTERS/Max Rossi. All rights reserved by copyright holder. May not be reproduced.

The image above the opening essay (page 7), a depiction of Mother Church in orans standing in a Romanesque church, was painted on the Barberini Exultet Roll, in Monte Casino, c. 1087. Currently in the Vatican Library. Wikimedia Commons: Mater Ecclesia.

The image for "Litanies and Laments" (page 10) is *The Paralytic* by Gisele Bauche. Copyright © Gisele Bauche, www.baucheart.com/gisele. Used by permission.

The image for "Thanksgivings at the Font" (page 28) is *Miriam* by Laura James. © 2006 Laura James, laurajamesart.com. Used by permission.

The image for "Thanksgivings at the Table" (page 37) is *Jesus Feeding the 5000* by Laura James. © 1999 Laura James, laurajamesart.com.